AMAZON FBA

Step by Step

A Beginners Guide to Selling On Amazon,
Making Money and Finding Products
That Turns into Cash

Red Mikhail

INCOME CLAIMS.

This is the part where I should put some income claims...so yeah, there you have it. NO INCOME CLAIMS. NO GUARANTEE OF EARNINGS. However, what I'm going to show you is the plan to possibly earn a full-time income via Amazon FBA Program… but then again, no income guarantees whatsoever. If you're fine with that, read on.

Also, *copyright material*...don't steal my stuff, you're awesome, write your own book :)

ONE MORE THING:

I am not going to promise you the world. I am not going to say that this is the only book you'll ever need for making money via Fulfillment by Amazon. That's crazy talk! The moment a guru or some schmuck tells you that, then run away as fast as you can!

Other Books by Red

FBA Product Research 101: *A First-Time FBA Seller's Guide to Understanding Product Research Behind Amazon's Most Profitable Products*

Amazon Associates Program: *Make Money Selling Amazon Affiliate Products Online*

One-Hour Dropshipping System: *Sell Physical Products Without an Inventory of Your Own*

Table of Contents

BONUS CHAPTERS

*For the 2021 update of this book, I added
2 chapters that can help you navigate the uncertainties of
the current marketplace.*

*I've added more or less 20 new pages of content and I
hope that you benefit from it. Thanks for supporting my
work and good luck!*

Introduction

Hey there my friend,

Thank you for purchasing this manual.

In this book, I'm going to show you a step by step plan on how you can make money selling products on Amazon via Fulfillment by Amazon (FBA). There's probably a million more ways to do it but I believe that if you follow the system that I will lay out to you, then you will make money.

Now, as much as I wanted to guarantee that you will make 1 million dollars, I won't.

Every business out there requires effort, a bit of investment and a lot of hard work to succeed. If you're in the Amazon FBA business to get rich quick, then I'm sorry to tell you but this is not the right place for you. However, if you're willing to take a few hours a day to work on your business, then you'll have a higher chance of succeeding.

Also, I wrote this book with the hope that it'll help guys like you quit their full-time jobs. If you already quitted and you're already making an income online, well congratulations! If not, this book has the potential to help you do it.

What can you expect from this book?

You should expect this book to be 90% actionable content. Most books out there about FBA are full of theories! They just want to get longer pages so they can sell their books at higher prices.

I'll be honest with you, as I am writing this, I have no idea if this book is going to be 60 pages, 90 pages or whatever.

What I do know is I'm going to put everything that you need to get started so you can have a good plan of attack for your business, and I hope that I can achieve that in this book.

Who shouldn't read this book?

If you don't have any sense of humour - yeah, just stop. I'm just some regular dude who want to share what he learned over the years. I'm laid back and I like to just talk like a normal person (that means cracking some jokes from time to time as well).

If you are an information collector, please, stop reading, this book is not for you. If you are afraid of taking a bit of risk and afraid of failure, stop reading as well, this book is not for you.

However, if you are ready to learn and implement, keep reading because this book is for you.

For you to understand the whole process much better, in the next chapter I'm going to give you a sort of 1,000 ft. overview of the system.

You're going to learn what to do first, second, third and on and on. Ready? Let's go!

1,000 ft. Overview

The Process in A Nutshell
(This will be your personal roadmap).

1. In chapter 1, we'll discuss how you can sign up as an FBA seller and the membership options available to you.

2. In chapter 2, I'm going to show you 4 ways to get started in FBA or what I call the plan of attack.

3. After the plan of attack, I'll teach you different methods to find products to sell.

This is the most important part of the book, I think you'll find lots of tips here that you won't get from any other book.

4. Once we received our product, we have to list it on Amazon. Also, we have to make sure that our product listing is fully optimized and will convert into sales. In addition, it won't be available for sale immediately because we still have to ship to Amazon fulfillment centers. That's where step 5 come in.

5. In chapter 5, I'm going to teach you what to do step by step to ship your product on Amazon and make sure that it'll be available for sale ASAP so you can start making money immediately.

6. You can't just rely on organic Amazon traffic, in the product listing part, we will do everything we can to make sure that your products will get found on Amazon, but it's not enough. We have to implement some traffic getting methods for you to get more eyeballs on your listings. You can actually skip this part if you like and go straight to step 7, but I don't recommend that you do it. Once you understand how powerful the traffic getting methods that I'm going to show you are. You'll be kicking yourself for skipping this step.

7. Reviews - Besides the traffic, reviews are the lifeblood of your business. it can make or break a product. Follow the guidelines that I'm going to show you to get more reviews on your products.

8. Rinse and Repeat - Once you got a hang of the process, you just have to rinse and repeat it. Find more products, sell more and make more money. Alright, let's start with the basics first. Chapter 1 is all about signing up as an Amazon Seller.

Chapter 1
Signing Up On
Amazon FBA

Let me give you a brief overview first just in case you're not familiar with FBA. Basically, it's like a done for you service where Amazon sells your products for you, they deliver it for you and they provide customer service for you.

Now, you can go to this link to sign up

http://services.amazon.com/content/sell-on-amazon.htm

You can sign up for free as an individual first. The individual account is for sellers who only have a few products to sell.

As an individual seller, you get charged $0.99 per product sold + additional fees instead of a monthly FBA membership.

You can always upgrade to professional by following the steps below.

Admittedly, I just copy paste that information from Amazon's forum.

1. Login to Your Amazon Selling Account

2. Go to Account Setting (Account Info)

3. You Will See the Selling Plan

4. Click Modify Plan

5. Click Upgrade

You Are Now Professional Seller On Amazon!

If you have any problems in setting up an account, I recommend that you call them immediately. I have found that they are more helpful when I get to talk to their customer service personally instead of email.

You can find more details about the pricing here:

https://sell.amazon.com/pricing.html

Amazon Fees - Terminologies and Meaning

Before we move on to the next step, I want you to get familiar with some of these terms so you don't get blindsided when these things come up.

1 – Referral Fee

This is what Amazon charge when they are referring customers to you, basically – it's a listing fee. It's usually 15% of the total product price but it varies by category.

2 – FBA Fulfillment Fee

This is the fee you pay for warehousing, delivery, returns, etc.

3 – Storage Fees

This is what Amazon charges for storing the products for you. There are monthly storage fees and there are long-term storage fees.

4 – Selling Fees

This is the upfront cost of doing business as an Amazon FBA seller. It's $39.99 per month or $1 per item sold.

Just know that the formula works like this:

Total fee = Referral + Fulfillment + Storage + Selling (fee). This is everything you need to pay to Amazon + the cost of your product + shipping cost and any other expenses.

Alright, it's time to choose our plan of attack.

Chapter 2
Four Ways to Get Started

You can choose any of these plans of attack that I'll recommend for you. There's no real right or wrong plan. It all works, it's up to you if you want to choose one over the others.

Also, these are not "official" ways to get started on Amazon, I just invented these myself, so yeah, follow at your own risk. (bwahaha, evil laugh)

Seriously though, these methods work. I won't write it here if it doesn't.

Way #1 - Top 100 Best Sellers

If it isn't broken, then don't fix it! If you chose this method, there will be more competition, but I'll try my best to help you beat them.

You can start by finding products that already sell well on Amazon.

To do this, go to

http://www.amazon.com/Best-Sellers/zgbs/

There will be TOP 100 items for different categories.

For Example:

Top 100 in Home & Kitchen
Top 100 in Kid's Home Store

You don't have to stick with the first page. Look also at the next few pages for product ideas.

Another thing that you can do is to find the top 100 under a category called sub-categories.

In the Kids' Home Store subcategory, you'll see *almost* the same products with just different pictures.

I am seeing a lot of "safety baby pads" that are selling like pancakes! They must be profitable and are selling like crazy. I'm not saying that you should sell baby pads, but if you keep seeing the same products pop up over and over again then it can be something to look at.

I'll be honest with you, it takes time to get a feel of the Amazon store, what sells well, what doesn't, what products gives more net profits, etc.

I suggest that you spend a minimum of 30 minutes a day shopping on Amazon and reading reviews. You don't really have to buy anything, just go "window shopping" and get a feel of the market.

Way #2 - Amazon Top 2,000

The top 2,000 can still be a gold mine especially for new Amazon sellers because it'll be less competitive. Most people skip the top 2,000 thinking that it won't make them any money. Big mistake! You can be the one who will take advantage of this.

The process is the same as finding products in the top 100.

So how do you do it?

It's a bit tricky but easy. Amazon doesn't have a top 2,000 list but what you can do is to type "[]"

on Amazon.com, choose a category and click search. Then you'll see over 400 pages of bestsellers in that category.

(Note: This doesn't work on all categories)

Scroll down to see the results.

You can go on Page 300 and those items will still be profitable!

Use this to get more ideas on what products to buy and sell.

Way #3 - Junk Products (Less than $10)

(They're not really junk, though I call them JUNK PRODUCTS)

These products could have a ton of reviews (or none at all - so they're a bit tricky) and are selling for very cheap. Usually, they are $1-$10 and below. Now, don't expect to get rich off these products but you can definitely make a full-time income just by focusing on them.

The name of the game for junk products is QUANTITY over quality. I'm not saying that your products should be literally junk, of course not. It should still be useful and people should like it.

Here's an example product. A Homelink Floral Zip Wallet for women.

[Image 2.1]

If you can sell a big quantity of these, especially if it's bulk, then it could be a big money maker. They're super cheap and has lots of reviews.

Way # 4 - Partner Up

If you don't have any capital but you have some skills about Internet Marketing (like SEO, Pay Per Click, Running FB ads), you can take advantage of your skill and partner up with someone already selling their products on Amazon.

You can find people who sell products on Trade Shows and even on Internet Marketing events about selling on Amazon! I highly suggest that you attend one, you'll meet a lot of businessman in these events.

If you want to learn more about internet marketing, you can follow a lot of gurus out there, be careful though! Some of these gurus will sell you on how easy it is to make money on Amazon. Don't be blinded by their shiny promises. Again, making a living in Amazon is very possible but it does take some effort and action.

Chapter 3
Finding Products

This is probably the most important chapter in this book. Why? because this is the part where most people give up! A lot of newbies have a hard time finding products that they can sell for a profit. I must admit, the beginning will always be the hardest because you still have to get a feel of your market. But once you are *"battle tested"* and more experienced, you'll find this step much easier.

I'm going to teach you six ways to find products. These are the same methods that I use every day in finding great ones that sell over and over again. You don't have to do all of them at once (that would be crazy), you just have to pick one and focus on that for a few days or weeks till you find a good product that you want to target.

The product that you will choose will always depend on how much you want to earn. If you want to earn $10 per sale, then you can't choose a product priced at less than $30. I found that the net profit (profit after advertisements, shipping, other fees etc) are usually at 30%-50% of the total gross sales. Don't be afraid to start small though.

Method # 0 - The non-obvious - obvious method + a note on Private Labels and how to find them.

You will hate me for even including this in the book, but it has to be mention.

The first method is by doing a google search, I know... duh..

But I see a lot of newbies don't do this. I have no freakin' idea why.

What you can do is to think of a product that you want to sell, say green juice powder. You simply type on Google "Green Juice Powder Manufacturer."

Another awesome search would be… "Green Juice Powder Suppliers" and my favorite… "Green Juice Powder *PRIVATE LABELS*"

The key here is to add the keywords: manufacturer or private label after your main product name.

The next thing that you should do is compile a list of manufacturers and then email or call them.

Not all will have what you need, or maybe the price is not right, whatever. Just continue to talk to manufacturers to also get a bit of experience in negotiating with suppliers.

On Private Labels...

Private labels are basically unbranded finished formula or product which you can brand as your own. You just have to choose the features that you want and put your own brand and VOILA, you now have your own branded product.

How to Find Private Labels

Method # 1 - Worldwide Brands
http://www.worldwidebrands.com/

WWB is a dropship directory, which means that they ship products to the end consumer directly. This means you don't have to worry about shipping your products to Amazon via FBA. WWB will ship your products for you directly to the end consumer.

(I'll still teach you how to FBA on the latter chapter - but for this method, there's no need for FBA)

Go on and register, it has a one-time fee of $299 and you'll have access forever. You can also pay via 3 months' instalment.

When you log in on your account, you'll see 3 different tabs.

It says, PRODUCTS - BRANDS - SUPPLIERS

I usually just go for suppliers and choose a category I am interested in. I then go through each supplier one by one and find some products

I can possibly sell. Once I found my potential product, I'll contact the supplier through the contact form. Contact as many as you can, not all of them will respond anyway.

In addition, you can also search for recently added suppliers. WWB adds different suppliers every now and then, this could be a great resource to find and test as many suppliers as possible.

Another awesome feature of WWB is the ANALYSIS tab. It's not super accurate but it gives you an idea of the competitiveness of that market.

Method # 2 - Alibaba (we're still on private Label Section) http://www.alibaba.com/ private-label-manufacturers.html

Alibaba is one of the most common ways to get Private Label Products.

The process is basically the same as WWB. You find a supplier, a product and contact them.

Beware though, some suppliers really suck...sorry, there's just no word to describe their products and services... it sucks. I'm not saying that you couldn't find a decent supplier on Alibaba, but I tend to find quality suppliers on WWB more often.

Here are some guidelines to follow for you to find great suppliers in Alibaba.

Response Rate

Transaction Level:	🔷 🔷 🔷
Response Time	24h-48h
Response Rate	55.3%

For the response rate, less than 60% is a big no-no!

Higher response rate means they actually care about their customers. I usually go with supplier's that has a response rate of 90% or higher.

Gold Supplier Badge

Some companies that has a gold badge tends to provide better products and better deals.

On-Time Shipment

You always want suppliers who ship their products on time.

If you really wanted to private label your products, I recommend that you spend a few hours talking to as many private label companies as possible. You never know when you're going to find the best deal.

Having a Private label product gives you an identity, a brand that you can market and build, which sells you more products in the long run. It does have a higher cost compared to just re-selling products first. If you're just getting started and have no cash. I suggest that you start with the 4th or 5th method that I will teach you.

CHEATSHEET - BEFORE YOU FINALIZE YOUR ORDER.

This is the exact cheat sheet that I use for my own e-commerce business. You should have the details for all of them before you go through the initial order.

You will get most of the details in the process of talking, researching and negotiating with your supplier.

1 – Name of Supplier

2 – All contact details (email, phone #, Skype etc.)

3 – Website

4 – Complete address

5 – Minimum order quantity (MOQ)

6 – What are their packaging and labelling options

7 – Do they do product customisation?

8 – Lead time

9 – Shipping Options/methods

10 – Price quotes for MOQ

11- Price quotes for packaging/labelling/customization

12 – The volume of product they can create every month

13 – How does shipping works and what are the fees (from Manufacturer's factory to your warehouse /Amazon FBA - DOOR TO DOOR)

14 – Are there any additional FEES for everything? (shipping, tax, customs)

15 – How does the quality control process works

16 – The exact weight, height and every single specifications of that product

17 – What payment methods will they accept? Most only accept T/T or wire transfer. Warning: Never ever pay via money transfer (Western Union). If they insist, run.

18 – Any possible third party options for shipping, packaging, labelling and product customization?

I know that all of these may sound a lot.

But if you come to think of it, 30% of the list can be answered through your own research. The other 70% can be answered in just two 15 minute phone calls!

Also, if you really want to stand out in this business, talk to them via phone/Skype and they will take you more seriously. When it comes to talking with suppliers, email is overrated!

You'll probably be uncomfortable talking to them in the beginning, but that's alright.

Would you rather be comfortable and broke?

Or would you rather be uncomfortable at the beginning and rich?

***

SUPPLIER PROCESS FROM A-Z

Here's the entire sourcing process from A – Z.

1- List all of your potential suppliers on your suppliers spreadsheet

On the first chapter, I told you about the different ways to find a supplier. Instead of contacting them immediately, what I'll do is make a list of suppliers first and put them on my spreadsheet.

You could also add a URL of where you found that supplier on your spreadsheet so it'll be easier to locate them just in case you need more details about that supplier or product.

2- Make first contact

ABP – Always be professional when you are talking or when you are emailing with these guys.

Also, act like a big and legit company. Even if you are just a "one man gang", introduce yourself as a product sourcing manager for your company.

When you make your first contact, make it as concise and as short as possible. Don't ask for price quotes or MOQ. They will give you all of these details when sooner or later.

Here's an example email I would send a supplier.

Hi,

My name is Red, purchasing manager for FreedomLife Inc.

We are looking for the best supplier for XYZ product name.

(productlink.com)

May I know who's the best person to talk to regarding this product?

I would prefer talking in SKYPE.

Here's mine: myskype.skype

Thank you,

Red

***

This is not as polish as I would like it to be but that's a good start.

Once they contacted you, set an appointment for a Skype call.

If they didn't respond, follow up over and over again.

Don't quit after 1 email. Follow up and separate yourself from other people who might try to do business with your preferred supplier.

3- Get Price Quotes

In your call, make sure that you get as many information as possible. Print your cheat sheet if you have to. Try to relax while talking to them, also **do not negotiate with price and moq just yet.**

4- Request Sample

If the numbers make sense then you should order a product sample and ask it to be delivered in your house/business address. Most of the time, they will ask you to pay a higher price per quantity and also pay for the shipping cost. Most items shouldn't cost you $100 (including shipping). This is normal practice because this will show them how serious you are in ordering this product. To get this expense back, I would suggest that you tell them that you would pay "that much" if they would credit the price of the sample to your initial order. 99% of the time, they would say yes.

5 - Negotiate MOQ

Here are some important things to know in order for you to negotiate a better price and lower MOQ.

A – Ask them the lowest quantity that you need to order in order to get the **absolute** best price. Aim for that price whatever your MOQ may be.

B – Always talk about building a long term relationship. Just like us, suppliers want to have recurring orders for their products.

C – Don't act needy, but don't act like an arrogant prick either. Just be confident when you talk to them, **act like a real professional who know what he's talking about.**

D – **Play suppliers against one another**. Tell them the MOQ and price that the other suppliers gave you. Send them proof if you have to, just make sure that you hide the details (company name and contact #) of the other supplier.

E – Sometimes, it's the best thing that they can offer. **Most companies have a threshold of what MOQ and price they can offer to a buyer.** If they really can't give you the price that you want, move on and find other suppliers. But don't burn bridges! Give them thanks and ask if they know other supplier that may have the product that you want. If they didn't reply, that's okay. At least you're not leaving them hanging.

6 - Place Initial Order

The last step is to place initial order. Know the following before finalizing your order.

1 – How many unit should you order

2 – What is the price per unit

3 – Where would they be shipped?

4 - What are the packaging and labelling options for your product

5 – Ask how does the whole process works - from A – Z. Remember to ask as many questions to your supplier as needed. Don't get lazy and assume that everything will go smoothly. If you don't understand something, don't be shy and ask!

On Shipping

Here are some terms that you need to familiarize yourself with when it comes to shipping your products. These are my "own" understanding and should not be taken as legal advice.

AWB – Air Waybill

This is basically a receipt or proof that you made a transaction with an airline, air carrier or air freight forwarder.

Bill of Lading

Same as AWB except that it's for sea transport.

Carrier

The business that is providing the service of transporting goods

FOB – Free on Board

This means that the supplier will pay the transportation of goods from their factory to the port (same country).

CIF – Cost, Insurance and Freight

If the supplier quoted a price with FOB & CIF, it means that they will also pay for insurance of product from their factory to the port.

EXW – Ex works (or FOB FACTORY)

You pay everything from FACTORY to port. **Do not accept Ex works type of deal.** They are just going to be a source of headaches. Skip the ex works!

***

So here's the 3rd method of sourcing a product.

Method #3 - Alibaba Reselling

Alibaba can also be used for reselling products.

For Alibaba, what I usually do is just go through different categories and find different products.

For example, I decided to go for *baby products*.

Now, on Amazon, I found a product that is selling quite well.

Puj Tub - The Soft, Foldable
Baby Bathtub - Newborn,
Infant, 0-6 Months, In-Sink
Baby Bathtub, BPA free, PVC...
More Choices from $42.99
★★★★☆ ▾ 539

I found a baby put tub that sells for $42.99. What you can do is find similar products on Alibaba. Again, it doesn't have to be exactly the same, but it has to be a good quality product.

The rationale behind it is that if people are buying that kind of product on Amazon, then you can probably sell the same "type" of product as well.

While searching on Alibaba, I also found a pub tub that is similar to the one I found on Amazon.

This one sells for $10 per piece when you order them.

You can probably sell it for $40 a piece on Amazon.

New Puj Tub - The Soft, Foldable
Baby Bathtub - Newborn, Infant, 0-...

US $10.00-$19.00 / Piece
50 Pieces (Min. Order)

Baby Store Mall

Just rinse and repeat the process. Not all products will be gold, you just have to keep digging and maybe you'll find one that will make you the most profit.

Method # 4 - eBay

One of the best ways to profit in Amazon is to find undervalued products on eBay. Some people might think that eBay is dying, Ha! they are wrong. There's still a lot of people making money on eBay. It might not be as profitable as before, but it's still a money maker for smart marketers.

What you can do is rebrand a product by taking better pictures on different angles and having better packages.

Also, don't be afraid to sort of change the strategy by buying on Amazon and selling on eBay instead. If you found an opportunity to profit, go on and take advantage of this. Some products are much cheaper in Amazon compared to eBay and vice versa.

How to find awesome products on eBay

Once you chose your plan of attack, go to eBay and find products that are similar to your chosen market.

Let's say I decided to go target "women's accessories" on the top 2,000.

I found this Stainless Bracelet on eBay selling for around $5 per piece.

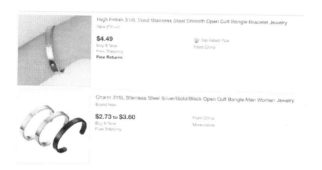

High Polish 316L Solid Stainless Steel Smooth Open Cuff Bangle Bracelet Jewelry
New (Other)

$4.49
Buy It Now
Free Shipping
Free Returns

Top Rated Plus
From China

Charm 316L Stainless Steel Silver/Gold/Black Open Cuff Bangle Men Women Jewelry
Brand New

$2.73 to $3.60
Buy It Now
Free Shipping

From China
More colors

What I'll do next is find similar products on Amazon that sells for a higher price.

Please note that it doesn't really have to be the same product. It just has to be a bit similar. If that product is selling on eBay, then it must be selling on Amazon as well.

I found an item below that looks similar to the one on eBay. It's selling for $19 and we can make a good $12 profit per item assuming that our product cost is $7. Not a lot but if you can sell just a piece a day, that's an extra $360 a month. It can add up pretty fast especially if you're selling a bunch of items in that niche.

Wistic Gold Cuff Bangle
Bracelet Stainless Steel Screw
Bar Bracelet for Women Men
Girls Boys
$17⁹⁹ - $19⁹⁹ ✓prime
FREE Shipping on orders over $25
shipped by Amazon
⭐⭐⭐⭐½ ▾ 23

Now, we are not sure if that item is going to make sales because it's not really a best seller, but still, I hope that you get the gist of the eBay method.

Here's another example.

Example search term is "remote control helicopter"

It sells for $90 on Amazon

Haktoys ATS S735C/HAK738C
2.4GHz Large 30" Video &
Photo Camera 3.5CH RC
Helicopter, Gyroscope,...
$89⁹⁵ ✓prime (4-5 days)
FREE Shipping
Only 7 left in stock - order soon.
Save 5% with coupon
★★★☆☆ ▾ 336

And on eBay, it's only $26)…$89 – $26 = $64 profit.

Do you think you could make a profit by doing this alone?

Of course.

Method # 5 - Walmart
http://www.walmart.com

Another awesome source of products is Walmart. It's cheap and they give free shipping. What I do is find sales and discounts and then make sure that there is a market for it on Amazon.

Example:

Expert Grill 17.5-Inch Charcoal Grill

★★★✦ 93

- 302 Square Inch Cooking Surface--Enough to grill 16 Burgers at Once
- Porcelain Firebowl and Lid
- Bottom Storage Shelf

$19.74

Free shipping on orders over $35
Free pickup

I found this Expert Grill with discount on Walmart

When I searched for charcoal grills on Amazon, I found the same product.

The one that I found on Amazon sells for $44. I would like to think that I can make a profit by buying the $19 product on Walmart (w/ free shipping) and then sell it on Amazon for $44 or more.

Here's another example. I found this one on the VALUE OF THE DAY tab.

Mainstays 14" High Profile Foldable
Steel Bed Frame, ...

★★★★⁴ 395

$50.00 - $90.00

This is a high-profile foldable steel bed frame.
It sells for $50 on Walmart.

And if you search on Amazon for...

"high profile foldable steel bed"

Mainstays 14" High Profile
Foldable Steel Bed Frame with
Under-Bed Storage
More Choices from $73.25

You'll see that it sells for $73.

Buy it for $50, Sell it for $73. Keep the profit and repeat!

I hope that I have expanded your imagination when it comes to finding products. It is probably the most important skills to master if you want to succeed in this business.

Chapter 4
Product Listing

So you found a product, ordered and received it. It's now time to sell it. For you to make a lot of profits, you have to create a product listing that really highlights the best features and benefits of your product. Also, it must be Amazon optimized so it'll appear much higher on the Amazon search engine.

Follow these simple guidelines to make your product listing is ready for action.

Photos

Always use high-quality photos. A bad photo will make your product appear unprofessional. In addition, only use white background for your product images.

Also, when uploading your pictures, change their file names into your keywords.

So if you're selling a helicopter toy on Amazon, change the image file name to helicopter toy.jpeg

Titles

Write detailed product titles. It helps in Amazon optimization and it makes your product stand out.

Instead of saying…

Helicopter Remote Control (Red)

Use a very specific name instead. Some like:

Axis Gyro RC Quadcopter with Camera RTF Mode 2 (red) - Easy to Use and Control - Even for Kids and Beginners

Make it detailed and also add some benefits.

So in our example, the benefits are - Easy to use and control - even for kids and beginners

Features are - *Axis Gyro RC Quadcopter with Camera RTF Mode 2* (red).. these are the physical attributes of the product.

Description

Never rush the creation of your description. By writing a thorough description, you'll be able to explain your product features and benefits much better. Also, it can help you rank in more keywords not included in your title.

In addition, take full advantage of the HTML amazon description feature. It helps in making your description look better since it changes font and size of your description.

Here are some basics that you can use.

B - BOLDS a phrase, used to define some words.
P - Defines a paragraph
BR - Adds a line break

Here's an example on how to use this on a listing.

<p><b> Why Choose This Product</b></p>

<p> - Discraft 175 gram Ultra Star Sport Disc</br>

-The world standard for the sport of Ultimate</br>

-Official and exclusive disc of the USA Ultimate Championship Series since 1991.</br>

-Listed among the 31 things all men should own by Esquire magazine</br>

-175 grams</br>

-Foil color on the disc will vary</p>

UPC Code

Amazon requires sellers to provide a 12-digit Universal Product Code assigned for every product. This was a huge problem in the past since not every supplier provides UPC.

To get the barcode as fast and as cheap as possible, go to one of these websites.

http://amazonupcbarcodes.com/

https://cheap-upc-barcode.com/

https://www.nationwidebarcode.com/purchase-barcodes/barcodes-for-amazon/

A WARNING (VERY IMPORTANT UPDATE FROM 2020 ONWARDS): Make sure that you do your due diligence. Some barcode companies do come and go and always double check if they have good service and positive reviews.

Chapter 5
Shipping via FBA
Step by Step

So you got your product sample, you've created your product listing draft and you're now 100% sure that this is the product line that you want to sell.

It's time to make your product available for sale via FBA and get it to Amazon's warehouse.

Here's the quickie of how it all works:

Step 1 - Send Your Product to an Amazon Fulfillment Center

-Go to your Amazon Seller Central and create your official product listing.
-Print the labels provided by Amazon or use FBA's Label Service.
-Use Amazon's shipping to get discount or chose your own carrier if you want

Step 2 - Amazon stores your products, now ready for shipping

-Amazon receives your product. They scan and measure your product.

-Using Amazon's integrated tracking system, you monitor your product inventory.

Step 3 - Amazon does everything else for you. The shipping, the customer service etc. Just make sure that you are enrolled on FBA program.

Check out this pdf provided by Amazon for a more detailed instructions:

https://images-na.ssl-images-amazon.com/images/G/01/fba-help/QRG/FBA-Shipping-Inventory-to-Amazon.pdf

This guide directly came from Amazon and it's the best technical guide you can follow. If the link didn't work, just simple search for "Amazon FBA shipping guide filetype:pdf" on Google and it should show as the first result in the 1st page.

Now let's talk about shipping: AIR VS. SEA

Unless it is already 3020 and we already invented a teleporting device, then we can only rely on 2 ways of shipping. AIR and SEA.

Here is my honest to goodness advice when it comes to choosing your shipping method.

Start with Air Express

Why? Because it's fast and it's simple. At first, your goal is to move as quick as possible. You need to test out products and you need to GO LIVE on Amazon so you can make your investment back and find out if this certain product really works.

That's not going to happen if you're waiting for 60 business days for your product to arrive at Amazon's facility.

Air Express are companies like UPS, DHL, and Fedex. Yes, they are more expensive – but they're also more reliable. Your product will usually arrive between 5-7 days.

This method is good for lightweight products and smaller type of shipments.

Cost may vary but it should be in between $5-$7 per kg.

SEA FREIGHT

If you are hell bent on saving money, then you can ship by sea.

In order to do this, you need to have a freight forwarder. Basically, a company that organize and handle all the tiny details that happen between shipping from your supplier to arriving at Amazon's facility.

Sea freight is good for heavier products and large shipments. And the cost may range from $150 - $350 per cubic meter. Think the size of 2 mountain bikes or the width of a two-seat sofa.

That's 1 CBM.

Want to find out the best forwarders to work with?

Join the Amazon Seller Central forum and ask other members for recommendation. You'll be amazed at how many sellers are willing to help you with this dilemma.

Extremely obvious, but HOT tip:

ASK YOUR SUPPLIER the best method for shipping as an AMAZON FBA SELLER. Most suppliers already deal with other sellers like you. They already know what to do – you just have to ask!

Sometimes, it pisses me off that new sellers will even hesitate to ask. They're afraid that it's going to make them look like a "newb" or an "amateur" – well technically (if you're reading this book), you probably are – so don't be afraid to ask.

Seriously, don't be "that guy" – much love though, I'm saying this for your own good.

How to Pay Your Supplier Without Getting Scammed!

A – Start with small orders. This way, you get to test whether they are competent and trustworthy or not.

B – The normal term is 50% deposit and then another 50% after pre-shipment inspection. But as you do more orders, it can be 30% upfront and 70% after pre-shipment inspection.

C – Use PayPal or Credit Card. Credit card is still the safest. Avoid Western Union, you'll probably get scammed if they insist in only using Western Union.

Pre-Shipment Inspection

Want to make sure that everything goes smoothly? Want to make sure that there isn't a panda bear hiding in your cargo?

Then go hire a 3rd party inspector who will do all the pre-inspection for you before the supplier ship the product. (You can also ask inside the Amazon seller's forum for recommendations on this).

What exactly does a 3rd party inspector do?

1 – They verify the quantity of the products (crucial).

2 – They make sure that the material and design is on par to your standards.

3 – They test the product and make sure that it's actually working. If they find product flaws, then the shipping won't push through and the supplier has to fix their shit. Sorry for the slightly vulgar

word, but that's exactly what the supplier has to do in this case.

4 – They check the shipment label and packaging.

Chapter 6
Getting Traffic

If you read my other book, Amazon Associates Program you'll be familiar with the tactics that I will teach you here. It's basically the same process except that we will send the "SEO POWERS, or BACKLINK" into our Amazon Product Link.

If you're quite lost and have no idea what I'm talking about, then don't worry. I'll explain this step by step.

NOTE: YOU WILL ALWAYS SEND THE BACKLINK (SEO LINKS) ON YOUR PRODUCT PAGE LINK.

To get the link, go to your Amazon Page and look at the upper side of your product listing. You'll see your unique URL, copy and save this on a text.

A. Ranking on Google

To rank your Amazon page on Google, we'll just hire someone on Fiverr to send a link to our URL.

Go to fiverr.com and search for "social backlink" or " high pr backlinks"

Get 4 different Fiverr gigs and send them the keywords that you want to rank for + your URL

Your keywords must include …

-Your product name
-Your product name + category

And you're done. Everything else will be done for you by your Fiverr freelancer.

B. YOUTUBE TRAFFIC

Another killer traffic source to use is YOUTUBE.

This is probably the easiest way to get traffic and sales to your Amazon page.

You'll simply hire someone to create a 5-minute video review of your product and upload this on YouTube. Make the video as simple as possible. Introduce the product, tell the pros and cons and ask for an action at the end of the video. Tell them to visit the link of your product (which you will put on your video description)

Here are the simple but important guidelines for uploading your videos. This is important for SEO purposes.

File Name

Change the name of your file to the keywords that you are targeting.

Properties

Change the TAG of your video, right click on your video and click details. Then add your keywords on the TAG part.

Title

Use a combination of your main keywords on the title.

E.g. *Red Helicopter Toy Amazon, Cheap Bracelet on Amazon*

Description

Try to make this as long as possible.

Explain what product you will review and why they should watch the video. This could be a short 1-2 sentences at the very least.

Tags

Put as many tags as possible. Your tags should let YouTube know that your video is about whatever your topic is.

Category

In the advance setting, change the category to whatever category suits your video.

Click Publish… and you're done!

How to Get Higher YouTube rankings?

This is really simple; I want you to follow the same process like the one I taught you in the RANKING IN GOOGLE section. The only difference is that you'll send your links to your youtube URL instead of the Amazon URL.

Chapter 7
The Importance of Reviews and How to Get Them

Reviews are the lifeblood of your products. Once you got positive reviews for your products, you can expect a boost in your sales. Also, it's important to get a few reviews first before officially launching your product to the masses.

Here are some ideas to get reviews.

Have a quality product

I know, I know... DUH, this is really obvious and common sense. But common sense is not so common these days. If you want to get a review then you should have a quality product.

Friends and Family

Giveaway your products to family and friends. Let them try the product for free in exchange for an honest review.

Now, be careful with this strategy. Your family members or friends should be from a different address or else, Amazon will ban your account. (Kindly check Amazon's terms since family members are not allowed to review the product - but it's a bit vague so you might as well read the whole thing). I'm only recommending this strategy for distant relatives and those who are a bit far from where you live.

Target Amazon Top Reviewers

A top Amazon review is always great for your product image.

How do we get them?

‾Go to http://www.amazon.com/review/top-reviewers

‾Choose a top reviewer and find someone who is reviewing a product similar to yours.

‾ Look under their profile picture to see if their contact information is public

‾ See their interests

‾ Contact them. Tell them how you found them and ask if they are interested in getting your product and reviewing it.

‾ Repeat the process a minimum of 10 times. Not all of them will agree to review your product, but once you got one top reviewer, then you are already ahead of the competition.

Giveaways

You'll get more positive reviews from people who bought your product through a giveaway. . (Again, please see Amazon's terms on this one).

Affiliate Marketers

There are people promoting products like yours on their own websites. Contact them and give them the product for free (if you can) and ask for a review.

To find affiliate marketers, just search your product on Google.

So let's say you are selling a green juice powder. You can find some affiliate by searching "green juice powder reviews."

Email them and ask for an Amazon product review.

(Make sure NOT to incentivise them with money as this is against Amazon's terms.)

Chapter 8
18 Best Practices

These are the practices that enable me to learn more about the business, find good products, choose great suppliers and ultimately make more money.

#1 - The 30 Minutes Habit

Every day, I spend a minimum of 30 minutes just browsing pages after pages of different products. By doing this, I am able to build my product and market knowledge. Also, this expands my knowledge about prices and what customers want in a product.

#2 - Don't Sell a Bad Quality Product

I never, ever sell a bad product. I don't care if it'll make me thousands of dollar up front. If it's not something I would personally use or something I would not recommend, then I won't sell it. Karma's a bit*h, you sell crap, crap comes back to you.

#3 - Diversify the product source

You don't have to import all of your products from different countries outside the U.S. Try different sources and find out what works for you.

#4 - Discount

Don't be afraid to ask for a discount.

#5 - Awesome Manufacturer

Once you found an awesome manufacturer, cultivate this relationship and make sure that you're both making a profit.

#6 - Trade Shows

Attend trade shows to get a feel of what people outside Amazon are selling. If people are buying it outside Amazon, then they will probably buy it inside AZ.

#7 - Traffic

Never rely on Amazon organic traffic alone. I taught you SEO and YOUTUBE, take advantage of this information and rank your Amazon pages on Google.

#8 - Keywords

Write keywords that not only sell the product but also keywords that optimized your product page for Amazon traffic and ranking.

#9 - Know the supplier personally

If the supplier knows you, he'll give you more discount and will make sure that they only ship quality products to you.

#10 - Photos

A good photo can double or even triple your sales. Invest in a good camera or hire a professional to take photos of your product. A white background always works great.

#11 - Product Listing

If your product listing sucks, no one will buy it. Review the product listing chapter over and over again, it's that important.

#12 - The Little Things

I think you already know that this business is not some kind of magic. There are no super secrets that will make you a millionaire. It's all a combination of doing the little things. Examples: Double checking your listings, making sure that you respond properly on a bad review, know what they want, what went wrong, etc.

#13 - Start Small

You don't have to start by selling products at $100-$500 price range. Start with products priced at $20-$30. This is the sweet spot when it comes to selling on Amazon for beginners.

#14 - Reviews

Always try to get a review from friends, family members, and current customers before making the official launch of the product.

#15 - Cut Your Losses

Some products won't sell as expected. No need to be a drama queen about this, cut your losses and move on.

#16 - Gift cards

You can set up coupons to give away to your friends and family members (gift cards). These discounts still count as an official sale thus making your product ranked higher on the bestseller list.

(Please see Amazon's term as this one is in the gray area side of things!)

#17 - Labels

Always double check the labels of your product and make sure that it's correct.

#18 - Shipping

Always go with free (or cheap) shipping on the products that you will re-sell.

Alright.

Hopefully, you'll follow these best practices. One tip alone if acted upon can make you thousands of extra income per month.

BONUS CHAPTER #1

THE PANDEMIC AND HOW IT AFFECTS YOUR FBA BUSINESS

There is no denying that the pandemic has completely turned our world upside down.

As of the moment that I'm writing this, there is still no mass-produced vaccine and millions of people already lost their jobs.

This is terrible and I feel for all those people. However, one thing that you probably didn't notice (or maybe you did?) is during this pandemic, Amazon's sales skyrocketed and billions of dollars were spent through online shopping.

THIS CHANGES EVERYTHING - FOREVER

Whether you're reading this in 2020, 2021, or 2030, this pandemic changes everything.

The pandemic forced people to change their buying habits. This means more people are shopping online than ever before. And don't think for a second that this buying habit will only be enforced during the crisis. This buying habit will stick and more and more people will continue to do their shopping online even after the virus disappears.

Opportunity

They say that more millionaires are made during an economic downturn than vice versa, and I have to agree to that.

If you know how to take advantage of a dire situation, then you will come out as a winner.

That's the mindset that I want you to have. To look at this awful situation and use it as a springboard to a better future.

Complaining and fighting with your friends on social media will do you nothing.

As selfish as it sounds, I want you to focus on yourself while you're starting your FBA business. If you do this, then I guarantee you that 12-18 months from now, you will come out as the winner.

Now, I want to give you some points to remember as you get started on this journey. Most of these are simple advice that will get you better results if you implement them.

So here are the 20 things that you need to look at as you start and grow your own FBA business:

#1 - Start Looking at Trends

The first thing that you should do is to start looking at trends. Are there any markets that suddenly skyrocketed in growth? Are there any industries that are just bleeding right now?

I recommend that you start with finding a product on Amazon and then using Google Trends to see if the searches for that type of product is growing or shrinking. You don't want dip your feet on that product category if it's shrinking in popularity.

At the very least, you want something that is consistent and is not in a downward trend.

#2 - Don't Get Boxed by the Trends

I know, I know - I just said start looking at trends and now I'm contradicting myself. Well.. not quite.

You see, most FBA sellers look at trends and then they get stuck in that pattern of thinking.

They start thinking that because a product is not trending, it means that it isn't making money.

Trends are a good starting point. But don't get boxed by the mindset that you always only have to sell trending products.

There is always a season for everything. That mega-trending product you found may not be that hot anymore 6 months from now. Who knows what's going to happen?

We live in uncertain times and relying on trends alone wouldn't get you far.

#3 - Personal Luxury Can Wait

If you have extra cash lying around right now, then don't spend it on personal luxury.

Instead, use that money to test out different products and different categories.

I know, it's super tempting to just splurge on new gadgets and bling bling. But if you can apply delay gratification, then you will come out stronger in the end.

#4 - Luxury Items Can Wait

Speaking of luxury, forget about selling luxury items during crisis/pandemic or any type of economic downturn.

Is there still a market for high-end products even on a recession and bear market? Absolutely.

So the question now becomes this: Can you afford to lose money while testing out your "high-end" product ideas?

Luxury items will most likely cost you higher manufacturing costs. This means if it doesn't work out, you'll lose a lot of money in the process.

Also, selling luxury or high-end items requires that you build a brand first. Even uber-luxury brands are hemorrhaging cash right now.

Forget about luxury items for now.

#5 - Start Using Facebook Ads

If you're not using Facebook Ads yet, then I have no idea what you're still waiting for.

Believe it or not, ads got cheaper since the pandemic happened.

Will the discount last forever? Of course not. But the more time people spend at home, the cheaper the ads become. This is a great opportunity for you and me to grow our e-commerce brand/s.

#6 - Think Long-Term

I can tell you that an awful lot of people will start their FBA business in the coming years and 99.9% of them will probably fail.

Not because they are bad with marketing or product research. But because most of them only think about short-term gain. Most will quit at the first sign of hardship and most people won't accept losing a little bit of money in the beginning.

If you're someone who easily gets disheartened, I'm afraid that this isn't the business for you.

I've wasted more money in my business that I'm proud to admit, but I never once thought about quitting and going back to a 9 to 5. If you have the heart of an entrepreneur, then quitting is not an option. Temporary setbacks are what I call them. There's always a solution and I'm always ready to find out what those are.

#7 - Start Building a Brand

If you're here for the long-term then there's only one way you're going to build a successful e-commerce business. It's by building a well-loved and respected brand.

When we say brand, that doesn't mean that you have to have some billion-dollar marketing machine and billions of people using your product.

NOPE.

It just means that you have to have a good product that your niche market loves to use. It means having extra customer support through other channels either via email or social media. FBA is good because you don't need to do any customer service. But to go to the next level, you have to provide an extra level of service to your customers, and having some kind of social media presence or company customer support does that for you.

In the next bonus chapter, I'll give you some of the best tips on how to grow an e-commerce brand.

#8 - Create a Product Line-up

All my life, I've suffered from dry skin. When I finally found a brand of body wash that works well for my body, I decided to try some of their other products. This company has shampoo, soap, foot wash, etc. Mind you, this isn't some big billion-dollar company. But when one of their products worked well for me, I decided to try out almost their whole line up. If they didn't have any other product aside from that body wash, I would've been a bit disappointed since I know that their stuff works.

If you want to build a successful e-commerce business, then you gotta have a product line-up in the same category.

You can't be running around with 5 products on 5 completely different categories. Can you make money doing this? Yes. Is it the ideal situation? No.

By building a product lineup on the same category, you'll make more money and you'll be able to build a brand that people love to use.

#9 - Mobile Shopping Will Be Unstoppable

Mobile shopping is growing and there's no stopping it. Almost everyone you know probably have a smartphone and they use it to shop online.

Amazon has a pretty easy interface when it comes to mobile shopping. They also have a simple app that's easy to use. It has big call-to-actions, predictive search, and great product pages.

What you can do is to make sure that you have a high-quality image and a properly formatted product listing to make it more Amazon optimized.

#10 - Online Grocery Is Big

More and more people are doing their family grocery online. This is a huge opportunity for us as we can try to sell items that fall under this category.

Don't think for a second that only big companies will benefit from this trend. It's not just food that people buy for their groceries. First, they buy the essentials and then they also do shopping spree for items related to family entertainment like board games, sports equipment, personal care, beauty products, furnishing, and home improvement.

#11 - Keep Educating Yourself

Learning never stops. That's the mindset that I've incorporated into my life over the years.

This means making sure that:

1 - I learn from my mistakes.

2 - I learn from other people's mistakes.

3 - I continually look at how the marketplace is changing.

4 - I keep reading books that will help me grow my business.

5 - I take some high-quality courses and talk to my mentor regularly.

Want to stay in this business for a long-time? Then promise yourself that you'll never stop learning.

#12 -Faster Shipping is Key

This is the biggest reason why you should use FBA. People don't want to wait 7-10 days for their products. They want to have it as soon as possible. That means 3 days at max.

If your product is already inside FBA, then you don't have to worry about this. Amazon got you covered already.

#13 - Non-Essential Travel Will Take a Hit... But It Will Make a Comeback

Travel related products (e.g. luggage, bags, pillows, passport wallet) will go down in sales.

So if you don't have the dexterity to stay in that category, then you better get out for now.

However, I do believe that it will make a strong comeback. Those who are willing to take a little bit of hit now will dominate this segment for the years to come.

#14 -Product Quality Trumps Everything

Look, there is nothing more important than this.

Selling knock-off products, copy-cats, and low-quality stuff can bring you short-term sales but it will ruin your brand's reputation.

If you're going to do e-commerce, you might as well do it the right way. That means selling quality products that your customers love to use.

#15 - Preppers Ain't That Crazy Eh?

Survival related products are actually on the rise. I'm not going to tell you what to sell but stuff related to prepping is killing it right now and will continue to do so for years to come.

Hint: Search on Google for "Prepper related products."

The preppers ain't that crazy after all.

#16 - Outdoor E-commerce Will Take a Hit... But It Will Make a Comeback + Gym Products Will Explode!

Products related to outdoor activities took a hit but most of these types of products will make a comeback. I'm not worried about this. I think fishing, hunting, outdoor sports, and other outdoor activities will rise again.

Also, you would think that gym related products are not in-demand anymore but it's the opposite. More and more people are buying workout-related products. The key is to find products that people can use in their house or apartment.

#17 - Home-Improvement Will Make Thousands of People Rich!

This is a trend that will make a lot of people rich. Everyone is buying stuff that can help them improve their home. Quite understandable since we're now spending more and more time inside the house.

When you go to Amazon for your product research, I recommend starting with the "Tools & Home Improvement" category.

Thank me later.

#18 - There's No Substitute for Hard Work

Most of the stuff that I talk about in this chapter are trends, techniques, or strategy. But no matter how great those things are, don't think for a second that they can replace good ole fashion hard work.

Remember, you still have to put in the work. You still have to outsmart and outwork your competition. While others are complaining about how everything sucks, you can be the person who will find solutions instead of worrying about the problems.

#19 - Adapt or Die

The marketplace is constantly changing and no one knows where it is going.

There's simply one rule that you have to follow to survive. It's either you adapt to the situation or your business will cease to exist.

#20 - Apply First Principles Thinking

First Principles thinking is a way of thinking critically and more deeply.

For example:

Let's say that I found a reliable data that says the "home improvement" category is growing by 20% per year.

I'll then ask myself the following questions:

1 - Is this true?
2 - Why?
3 - If it's true, how can I use this in my business?

By asking myself these questions, I'm forcing myself to think critically about the data. By doing this, I'll also be able to know what steps to take so I can take advantage of the situation.

***

A Warning.

Here's the truth: I could be wrong in some of these and only time could tell that.

Make sure that you do your research and make your own educated guess on the next steps that you have to take.

BONUS CHAPTER #2

BUILD A BRAND, NOT AN EASY-CASH MACHINE

In your pursuit of making a good living from FBA, you will be tempted to take shortcuts. You will be tempted to choose products that you think will make you quick cash. You'll be tempted to sacrifice quality for profits.

This is a normal feeling to have especially if you're a beginner seller. But I do hope that you'll grow out of this dangerous short-serving mindset.

To build a thriving Amazon business, you have to have the mindset of a brand-builder and a value creator.

Here are the top 10 mindset shifts that you need to make to succeed:

#1 - Focus on Product Quality

I'm not going to sugarcoat this. Quality products will always cost you more in manufacturing costs.

But is it worth having smaller margins just so you can get a higher quality product in the market? Damn, right it is.

In the short-term, you will make less money than your competition. But building a brand they can trust will lead to long-term success. They will buy and use your product over and over again. They will recommend it to others and you will have an army of people who are willing to promote your products for free via word of mouth.

#2 - Create Your Brand Assets

You must also exist outside of Amazon. Make sure that you also create a professional website and a consistent social media presence.

Start with creating your Facebook fan page as it's the simplest thing you can do to let them know that your company is legit.

After that, create a website where they can read more about your company and your products. You don't necessarily have to sell the product there. You can just link them out to Amazon where they can buy it.

#3 - Product Images is Key

I hope that this is pretty obvious by now. Always hire a professional photographer for your product images.

This is an absolute must!

#4 - Post Videos of Your Product on YouTube

If you can show people how your product works, then they are more likely to buy it.

It doesn't have to be a product review. It can just be you using the product or showing its features.

I found that doing this gives me an extra 20-50 sales per month per product.

Just make sure that you target keywords directly related to the one you are selling.

#5 - Listen to Feedback Reviews

Make it a habit to listen to customer feedback and always read your Amazon reviews with an open mind. Instead of being livid about your 1 or

2-star reviews, try to listen to their complaints and what they didn't like about the product.

Negative reviews can act as the feedback machine that you use so you can improve your product. Read the reviews religiously and analyze if they are valid. If they are, then make sure that you incorporate the changes needed to improve your product.

#6 - Sell Other Stuff

If you want to build a brand, then you gotta have a product line up. In the words of my mentor that you will never meet, "Just sell em' some other stuff."

Having a line up gives you more opportunities to sell them, which then makes you more money! Don't ever feel guilty about selling them more stuff! If they want and need it, then they will buy it. It might as well come from your brand!

#7 - Packaging is Branding Too

Good packaging is an investment in your product and your brand. It's the first thing that they will see once they open the package. And I can tell you from experience that first impressions last.

You have to make the numbers work. But make your packaging as good as possible without losing your profit margin.

#8 - Fast Shipping is the Best Shipping

Most people are impatient. So faster shipping is always better.

If you are still using old and tired shipping companies, then you already know what to do.

Just go use FBA and let them do it faster for you.

#9 - Add Extra Product Features

Always think about what the customer needs.

What extra feature can you add that will do the following?

A - Make using the product easier.

B - Make the product do something that it can't do before.

Do those 2 things and you'll easily add features that your customers will love and appreciate.

#10 - Go Beyond FBA

If you're keen on building a brand, then you have to expand beyond Amazon.

Now, you don't have to do this in the beginning. You are starting with FBA for a reason. But once you start making money, then you should start investing in your platform.

Building a trusted brand takes time and you have to go through some growing pains along the way. Accept that it will be hard and just work through it.

Conclusion

Woah! You finished the book, congratulations!

90% of you will never take action on what you just learned. That's a fact.

I know, that's quite sad and depressing.

My question to you is this. Do you want to be part of the 90% or the top 10% instead?

The choice is yours to make.

Follow my advice, re-read the book if you need to.

This is not a book that you read once and then leave to collect dust.

Make this your reference in your business and always make sure that you learn from your mistakes. Yes, you will make mistakes. That's a guarantee, your job is to learn from it and hopefully find a way to profit from that mistake.

Good luck in your journey and I wish you all the success in your AMAZON FBA business. I already showed you the steps, it's time for you to take action.

All the best,

Red

P.S. - There's a favor on the next page :)

Review Request

If you like this book and it helped you in some way or another, kindly post a review on Amazon.com. Reviews are the lifeblood of every author out there and it helps in sharing the message. I appreciate you and I look forward to hearing from you soon. Good luck with your business and I wish you all the success in the world.

Other Books by Red

FBA Product Research 101: *A First-Time FBA Seller's Guide to Understanding Product Research Behind Amazon's Most Profitable Products*

Amazon Associates Program: *Make Money Selling Amazon Affiliate Products Online*

One-Hour Dropshipping System: *Sell Physical Products Without an Inventory of Your Own*

Printed by Amazon Italia Logistica S.r.l.
Torrazza Piemonte (TO), Italy

17689396R00062